Muscular
Music

Muscular Music

Terrance Hayes

Carnegie Mellon University Press
Pittsburgh 2006

ACKNOWLEDGMENTS

Sincerest gratitude to the editors of following journals and anthologies in which some of these poems first appeared (sometimes in different versions):

African-American Review: "When The Neighbors Fight"

Beyond the Frontier: Anthology of African-American Poets: "What I Am," "Midnight"

Controlled Burn: "At Pegasus"

Cream City Review: "Jumpschool"

The Exchange: "Morning Poem," "Noir: Orpheus"

5AM: "Poet Dying At the Window," "Mr. Mouse Plays the Blues," "Salami"

Green Mountains Review: "Boxcar"

HeART: "Derrick Poem (The Lost World)"

The Iconoclast: "Shafro"

Identity Lessons, Poetry Anthology: "Late"

Nu Voices: "Blackbird"revision reprinted from *Obsidian II*

Obsidian II: Black Literature in Review: "Blackbird"as "I Call My Brother To Hear Roberta," "Something for Marvin"

The Pittsburgh Quartely: "Summer,""Ballad of Bullethead," "Buy One, Get One"

The Pittsburgh Post Gazette: "HOWYOUBEENS," "Pittsburgh"

Poet Lore: "Goliath Poem"as "The Sound Of A Big Man"

Red Brick Review: "Lady Sings the Blues"

The Shooting Star Review: "Hathaway"as "Song"

Special Thanks to: James and Ethel Hayes, the Pittsburgh crew (especially Toi Derricotte, Ed Ochester, and The Kuntu Writers Workshop); the DC crew (especially big brotha, DJ Renegade), Elizabeth Alexander (for this), and the Cave Canem Family (Yona, I found you).

Muscular Music was first published by Tia Chucha Press in 1999.

The publisher expresses gratitude to James Reiss and James W. Hall for their contributions to the Classic Contemporaries Series.

For Spanky,
my brother,
my brother.
I can't say it enough.

a lover

in no particular hurry,

the music reveals itself

a negligee black note at a time.

— Rueben Jackson

Table of Contents

AT PEGASUS

They are like those crazy women
    who tore Orpheus
        when he refused to sing,

these men grinding
    in the strobe & black lights
        of Pegasus. All shadow & sound.

"I'm just here for the music,"
    I tell the man who asks me
        to the floor. But I have held

a boy on my back before.
    Curtis & I used to leap
        barefoot into the creek; dance

among maggots & piss,
    beer bottles & tadpoles
        slippery as sperm;

we used to pull off our shirts,
    & slap music into our skin.
        He wouldn't know me now

at the edge of these lovers' gyre,

   glitter & steam, fire,

      bodies blurred sexless

by the music's spinning light.

   A young man slips his thumb

      into the mouth of an old one,

& I am not that far away.

   The whole scene raw & delicate

      as Curtis's foot gashed

on a sunken bottle shard.

   They press hip to hip,

      each breathless as a boy

carrying a friend on his back.

   The foot swelling green

      as the sewage in that creek.

We never went back.

   But I remember his weight

      better than I remember

my first kiss.

   These men know something

I used to know.

How could I not find them
    beautiful, the way they dive & spill
        into each other,

the way the dance floor
    takes them,
        wet & holy in its mouth.

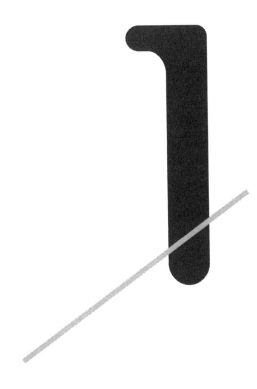

14

WHAT I AM

Fred Sanford's on at 12

& I'm standing in the express lane (cash only)

about to buy *Head & Shoulders*

the white people shampoo, no one knows

what I am. My name could be Lamont.

George Clinton wears colors like Toucan Sam,

the *Froot Loop* pelican. *Follow your nose,*

he says. But I have no nose, no mouth,

so you tell me what's good, what's god,

what's funky. When I stop

by McDonalds for a cheeseburger, no one

suspects what I am. I smile at Ronald's poster,

perpetual grin behind the pissed-off, fly-girl

cashier I love. Where are my goddamn fries?

Ain't I American? I never say, *Niggaz*

in my poems. My ancestors didn't

emigrate. Why would anyone leave

their native land? I'm thinking about shooting

some hoop later on. I'll dunk on everyone

of those niggaz. They have no idea

what I am. I might be the next Jordan-

god. They don't know if Toni Morrison

is a woman or a man. Michael Jackson

is the biggest name in showbiz. *Mamma se*

Mamma sa mamma ku sa, sang the Bushmen

in Africa. I'll buy a dimebag after the game,

me & Jody. He says, Fuck them white people

at work, Man. He was an All-American

in high school. He's cool, but he don't know

what I am, & so what. Fred Sanford's on

in a few & I got the dandruff-free head

& shoulders of white people & a cheeseburger

belly & a Thriller CD & Nike high tops

& slavery 's dead & the TV's my daddy—

      You big Dummy!

Fred tells Lamont.

MORNING POEM

After *Charlie Rose* where a man claimed proof
God is human, I hump the ten minute hill
to catch the 61C which arrives two minutes after
the rain and carries me without O'Hara or the blue
umbrella hanging on my closet door to Pamela's
on Forbes where I'm surprised to see K above a plate
of pancakes in a corner by a window, outside which
rain is kissing the heads of beautiful and ugly passersby

I join her, order ice-water and the Early Bird Special
at $4.87 after taxes and mention how long it's been
since I've seen her but not the fact she looks beat
and the webs through her hair kind of scare me
or that I expected bandages to brace her razor-prone
wrists and we don't explain how we came to eat alone
but talk about what it means to be *on the wagon* which K
is, how the news said nothing about rain, and I bring up
Frank's dumb dune-buggie death and the poems
I left on the chair by my bed as I eye the pack of Marlboro
Lights and damp matches by K which means we're in
the smoking section and nothing makes sense because
the windows don't open and Pamela's is only a tiny room
with soaked breathing people like us

By the time I finish the Early Bird, K has split

and I follow but she's long gone so I wait for my bus

in the rain which is not like a kiss, but a baptism

cleaving to my brown skin and the t-shirt

I stole off my father who smoked *Kools* on the steps back

home, and grew too fat to wear it

SHAFRO

Now that my afro's as big as Shaft's
I feel a little better about myself.
How it warms my bullet-head in Winter,

black halo, frizzy hat of hair.
Shaft knew what a crown his was,
an orb compared to the bush

on the woman sleeping next to him.
(There was always a woman
sleeping next to him. I keep thinking,

If I'd only talk to strangers . . .
grow a more perfect head of hair.)
His afro was a crown.

Bullet after barreling bullet,
fist-fights & car chases,
three movies & a brief TV series,

never one muffled strand,
never dampened by sweat—
I sweat in even the least heroic of situations.

I'm sure you won't believe this,

but if a policeman walks behind me, I tremble:

What would Shaft do? What would Shaft do?

Bits of my courage flake away like dandruff.

I'm sweating even as I tell you this,

I'm not cool,

I keep the real me tucked beneath a wig,

I'm a small American frog.

I grow beautiful as the theatre dims.

DERRICK POEM (THE LOST WORLD)

I take my $, buy a pair of very bright kicks for the game

at the bottom of the hill on Tuesday w/ Tone who averages

19.4 points a game, & told me about this spot, & this salesman

w/ gold ringed fingers fitting a $100 dollar NBA *Air Avenger*

over the white part of me—my sock, my heel & sole,

though I tell him *Avengers* are too flashy & buy blue & white

Air Flights w/ the dough I was suppose to use to pay

the light bill & worse, use the change to buy an Ella

Fitzgerald CD at *Jerrys*, then take them both in a bag

past salesmen & pedestrians to the C where there is a girl

I'd marry if I was Pablo Neruda & after 3, 4 blocks, I spill out

humming "April in Paris"while a lady w/ a 12 inch cigar

calls the driver a facist cuz he won't let her smoke on the bus

& skinny Derrick rolls up in a borrowed Pontiac w/ room

for me, my kicks & Ella on his way to see *The Lost World*

alone & though I think the title could mean something else,

I give him some skin & remember the last time I saw him

I was on the B-ball court after dark w/ a white girl

who'd borrowed my shorts & the only other person out

was Derrick throwing a *Spalding* at the crooked rim

no one usually shoots at while I tried not to look his way

& thought how we used to talk about black women

& desire & how I was betraying him then creeping out

after sundown with a girl in my shorts & white skin

that slept around me the 5 or 6 weeks before she got tired

of late night hoop lessons & hiding out in my crib

there at the top of the hill Derrick drove up still talking,

not about black girls, but dinosaurs which if I was listening

could have been talk about loneliness, but I wasn't,

even when he said, "We should go to the movies sometime,"

& stopped.

SALAMI (A MANIFESTO)

"in these modern times when people
have to be disturbed, so terribly terribly disturbed
just to be interesting i just want to be normal,
like a brown-eyed handsome man"
　—Jerome Sala

I.

My mother works third shift in a men's prison.

Mornings she unlocks my bedroom door

& says: *It's 6 am, Have you fed*

the dog yet? 　I think I'd like to be

(a) a prison guard. I'd carry a dozen clattering

silver keys and where striped pants.

If I couldn't be a prison guard (I have bad

credit), I'd like to be (b) a stripper

named Disco Dick. 　I've told you this before,

I'd have salami stuffed down my studded

g-string. I'd do the butt-naked hustle

for middle-aged accountants with bus tickets

II.

in their fists. (Accountants get nudity

where they can.) (Bus tickets give entrance

to the soul.) As a stripper, I could write

poetry all the day: *O my Love is a Redhead*—

Rose. (c) I could even moonlight

as a prison-stripper guard, dance

for the unaccountables —COMMERCIAL BREAK—

Rose calls from home. Instead of poetry

or geometric equations, I suggest phone sex.

"What are you wearing,"I ask. "I'm thinking

about your breasts," I say. "Are you reciting

a poem or something?" she asks.

III.

I come with the mathematic efficiency of Sir

Issac Newton. Dear Elmer Fudd, I have lost

a damn good woman, and no longer want to live.

Can I borrow your gun? Sincerely, (a) Ernest

(b) Kurt (c) insert name.

If I was a lonely housewife, I'd dye my hair

five times a week. (Mondays) flamingo

pink (Tuesday) fool's gold (Wednesdays) casper

IV.

white (Thursdays) mood indigo (Fridays) camouflage.

Can you tell I'm wearing a wig? America means:

passengers will surrender

their tickets to the driver upon leaving the bus.

I am a brown-eyed and private dick, be careful

how you love me. Where are you going

with my salami? Hey, god-dammit, I'm talkin

to you! Oh, well, never mind. Dear poet,

V.

you are normal and that is why you must die.

Please remember to feed the dog.

I'll be by after breakfast. Love,   (a)

(b)

PITTSBURGH

is a fat lady jabbering at the bus stop.

She mistakes me for someone who gives a damn,

For a native son of her gray industrial breast.

She blesses her Bucs, her Steelers,

Her father, *God rest his soul,* was a Hornets fan.

She mistakes me for someone who gives a damn,

Her blue scarf twisting like the broad Monongahela,

Her blue face lined like a jitney's street map.

I'd tell her I'm not from this place:

These severed tired neighborhoods,

These ruthless winter tantrums,

But her long winded stories numb me.

She is persistent as snow, as boot slush & concrete,

As buses rumbling like great metallic catepillars.

She lights a Marlboro and it means

Spring will burn quick and furious as a match,

Summer will blaze.

When she tells me *No one is a stranger in Pittsburgh,*

do I believe her,

My frosty fairy foster-Mamma,

My stout rambling metaphor?

BUY ONE, GET ONE

The old white man reading a box of *Corn Flakes* is like me.
Do you ever get up to go no where at sunrise? I shop at dawn
before all the good eggs are cracked. Only I & the elderly
know the super market is last vestige of America—
namebrands & generic condiments, blackeye peas, white rice,
spanish onions— everything has its cost. This morning
it's *Aint Jemima's Authentic Maple Syrup With Artificial Flavoring*,
BUY 1, GET 1 FREE. Meaning, one's half as much as usual
& I'm getting something for nothing. The cashier
has two bouyant breasts to compensate for her lack
of arithmetic. She hands me my change one coin at a time
as if I can't count. How much do I deserve?
In the 10th grade I knew briefly numbers to be the Grand
Daddies of the Cosmos. Pythagoras & Plato, knew it too—
MATH: realm of the Real & Infinite Truth. Each old man
was right to scorn poets for their noise about Death
& personal Beauty. Anyone will tell you, Poetry
is beautiful, but it ain't no super Model. Greeks had Logic
to compensate for their lack of Romance. Still, the Supermarket
with her aisles of cubes & cylinders & $3.14 cent pies
dons a kind of elegaic splendor. One plus one can equal one,
because, BUY 1, GET 1 FREE, means: 1 is Indivisible—
One Nation, with Liberty & Justice etcetera.
"Buy one, get one free," said the slave trader to cotton heads
when pregnant African girls mounted the auction block. America!
Everything has its price; nearly everything has been bought.

I WANT TO BE FAT

I want to be fat,
I want a belly big enough to hold
A refrigerator stuffed with trout,
Big enough to house a husband with a beer gut,
A wife with a baby in her belly.

I want to be fat like a Volkswagon bug,
Candy-apple red, or cabbage green
With a burping engine and curving hood
Which opens to reveal my penis tucked
Safely between the crowbar and spare.

When I am fat,
Ladies sipping diet colas will whisper:
Look at him. My God how'd he get so big?
And beneath those questions they'll think,
I wonder if he still makes love?
I wonder what he looks like naked?

Love me skinny girls,
As you love jenny craig and vegetables,
Love me fat girls,
As you love insecurity and everything filling.
I'll let you kiss my triple chins,
I'll let you swim in the warmth of my embrace.

When I am fat
I'll scramble a dozen eggs each morning,
Brush my teeth after every meal
—this, of course, in the years
Before I am eight-hundred pounds,
Before I marry my mattress,
And lay all day swallowing
The light of tabloid TV.

I'll cry elephant tears
When *Cooking with Betty Crocker* is cancelled,
I'll curse flexing biker-shorts and ESPN,
And I'll never forget you, Fat Albert,
Your ass like heaving pistons of flesh,
Your stomach like a massive tit
Beneath your tight red shirt.

"You motherfuckers will have to give me
My own seat on the bus!"

I want to be the champion of excess,
The great American mouth with perfect snapping teeth,
I want fat children to send me letters
Of self-love and gratitude,
I want to swell thick with love and gratitude.

I want to be buried in an ocean of dirt,

This ocean of flesh, this heart

Like a fish flopping at the center of it;

This heart like a skinny man gasping

at center of it;

This heart. This heart. This heart

HOWYOUBEENS

Mostly people talk to people, standing
Round to jibber-jabber in the blue hours
Of weekdays. You see them meandering
Words while the calendar tilts and pours
Its steady juice of minutes. You see them
On Forbes almost vaporish, almost stupid
To newspaper's steady whip; to trash bins
Gluttoned with dollheads, switchblades, red-lipped

Cups, obituary ink, love letters,
Teeth of hair-combs, relics of the moment:
Everything ignored in the name of Weather,

Of somebody's business & "Howyoubeens."
I too am guilty. Chattling after strangers.
Wasting it. Dumb. Bitching about the wind.

SUMMER

In Oakland a white girl sings
what sounds like the blues,
song Summertime splashing
in her throat & I start thinking
I'd like to sing it too: a classic.
But nowadays brothers don't sing
the Gershwin tune,
a white man's vision
of plantation paradiso:
pretty black Bess, pickaninnies.
Porgy and thick cotton coons.
Enough is enough.

It's Summer so I hum.
Let bass slip around
my runagate tongue.
I have lived watermelonless,
I have scorned my languorous youth.

These days, I listen too closely
to your music, deaf
to the pit & patter of Politic.
O Summer, let me sing a song for you,
Let me be the king of something,
O Summer, let me spread my wings

The Yummy Suite was inspired by events in Chicago the summer of 1994. Eleven year old Robert "Yummy" Sandifer murdered fourteen year old Shavon Dean while firing on a rival gang. All italicized remarks are taken from the article written by Nancy R. Gibbons and reported by Julie Grace and Jon D. Hull in the September 1994 issue of Time magazine (Volume 144, Number 12).

BALLAD OF BULLETHEAD

I was born in metal

    —my mother's kettle

  My father peddled

     So we settled alone

Metal child & mother of stone

    Another story of moans

  Bank loans Shut off telephones

Thru spring & winter storms

    In my body of arms

  Carry charms of speech

     Tires screech Preachers preach

"The world is full of harms"

    The man you couldn't reach

     Mud hunger to eat

O say can you see

    Street corner to street

  Pantomime of feet

     But I'll beat uncle sam

& I won't give a dime or a damn

    & my willows won't weep

  Tho the dead are asleep

     And my mother's a pillow

Of grief

Bullethead is who

I be

O say can you see

Words sounding absurd

But I gotta get heard

On corner On curb Car garage Back yard

—Lyric fusillade

Sentence propensity This word—

world intensity Past

tense Ten pence

Whatever makes cents

Cause I can't pay the rent

Pennies spent in my pockets

Pennies bent in my fist

& my body's a mist

& my body's a smog

What I mean is

My body's the dark

& my tongue is a spark

& the light will dismiss me

Cause my words make it woozy

& the anger has bruised me

But my mouth's screamin Choose me

And my heart

Is a boy

Who's dizzy

YUMMY SUITE
BLUES

Yummy spent the last 3 days
of his life on the run.

***

Sun out like a floodlight.

Does it burn?

Watch on your wrist like a cuff.

Does it run?

You stole your sneakers

& a fistful of sweets.

Here come the Death Rush.

Hit the road!

Slip into the alley

Like a burning bush.

What happens when a dream explodes?

Does it hush?

YUMMY SUITE
BLUES FOR SHAVON

Shavon lived around the corner
from Yummy and had known him growing up.

***

Shouldna been playin
On that corner anyway
Pavement was hot,
Potholes everywhere,
Bottles everywhere.
Those streetlights flickered on
And your little ass shoulda been home,
Steada tryin to be so grown,
Makin the big girls see you,
Makin the bad boys howl & moan . . .

Watched you dance & double-dutch,
Watched you shake & shimmy,
Watched the bullets hopscotch.
Damn, the scattered crowd,
Your scattered smile, your rag-doll flop.

Lord, you shouldna been there, Baby.
And he shouldna been there.
Lord he shouldna been there, Baby. . .

YUMMY SUITE

From Reen

Yummy's mother, Lorina called him
without irony an average 11-year old.
He shouldn't be dead, she says sitting
in her living room the day after his funeral.
There is a white bucket in the corner
with a live frog he caught a few weeks ago.

    ***

Boy,

you interupted my conversation
bustin through the door
with that goddamn frog

Drivin me out my fuckin mind

I'm tired of talkin to you

Nigga, you just won't listen

Bought me eleven years trouble
Eleven years grief

When they find your ass dead,
Hope they don't call me

YUMMY SUITE

JANIE FIELDS

Janie Fields last spoke to Yummy the Wednesday afternoon
before he died. He said, *What is the police looking for me for?*
I said, *I'm coming to get you.* I had clothes with me 'cause I knew
he was probably filthy and dirty. My heart was racing. I said,
You ain't done nothing wrong, just let me come and get you.

***

At the corner of 95th street
she thinks of her telephone ringing
and ringing with no one home

to answer, the T-shirt like a ghost
in her fist. A siren sweeps by,
but she does not think

of her grandson. When she gets the news
she does not fall down. She does not tremble
returning his shirt to the drawer.

YUMMY SUITE

FROM MICAIAH

Yummy liked great big cars, Lincolns and Cadillacs,
says Micaiah Peterson, 17. *He could drive real well.*
It was like a midget driving a luxury car. Sometimes he hung

***

Everybody asks if I knew you

I say, Yeah

And sometimes, I lie.

I say, Nothings changed since Yummy died,

People still bullshit on the corners

Sunset to sunrise.

I say, You'd cruise by in a Caddy

And niggas' eyes popped with disbelief,

They'd laugh and holler after you,

Beggin for a ride up the street.

     ***

out at the local garage, learning about alternators and fuel
injectors. When he wasn't stealing cars,
he was throwing things at them or setting them on fire.

YUMMY SUITE

LOCAL GROCER

He was a crooked son of a bitch, said the local grocer

who had barred him from the store for stealing so much.

Always in trouble. He stood on the corner and strong armed

other kids. No one's sorry to see him gone.

***

Not catching the little crook on aisle four,

Not dragging the T-Shirt—

Not the body in the shirt,

Past produce to barred doors,

Not the mothers, not the bangers, not Shavon.

The grocer remembers nothing:

His linoleum floors are mopped

(Not the spill),

His customers shop

(Not the faces, not the names),

Over five-hundred items in his store,

He knows the price

Of everything.

YUMMY SUITE

LITTLE RON

What exactly did he look like?
Kind of like he was gone, you know?

When Mamma pushed me foward
I thought I was going to fall
right in the damn coffin.

***

The whole church smelled like a toilet,
if that's what you want to know.
Wasn't sweet cause none of the flowers was real.
Yummy suit was too big.
His eyes was stitched for good.
I backed away.
"They need to bury him in that sewer,"
I heard a lady say.
None of them flowers was real.
I went outside & saw a man in the ground
where the sewage pipes had broke.
I wasn't cryin if that's what you want to know.

YUMMY SUITE

DERRICK & CRAGG

Derrick Hardaway, 14, and his brother, Cragg, 16,
both honor students and fellow gang members, found Yummy
and promised that they could help get him out of town.

***

Do you think of Shavon

When they take you to the underpass

Do you think of ketchup splattered shoes

And pockets full of rocks

Bullets furrowed like seeds

When they knock you down and blast

When your face unravels like a bruise

Do you think of Shavon

Do you think of Shavon

JUMPSCHOOL

...the high came when you found you'd landed safely
—Jimi Hendrix, 101st Airborne

Today there is no war,
    only this crowd of people,
        green and idle as weeds,
watching the helicopter rise:
    My parents, fatally proud
        & camera-ready,
crewcut medics smoking

by an ambulance, a few boys
    wrestling in the grass.
        I remember reading
Jimmy Hendrix left jumpschool
    with bad ankles & a cheap
        guitar, and think now
of the few wild years he lived

teasing Death the way he'd tease
    his fans: singing loud on manic
        knees; acid bobsledding
his veins, fingers & teeth
    strumming Stratocastor flames.
        I am trying to understand danger:

those summers my baby-brother

backflipped from diving boards,
    and the wheel of his body
        turned me dizzy;
those nights he was reckless
    on roller-coasters twisting
        like barbed wire
across amusement parks.

Now, as soldiers fall
    from the chopper, banging
        their helmets on sun,
rocks in an odd constellation,
    I feel the earth beneath my shoes.
        Their chutes open wide
as Hendrix's giant hands,

around me, people begin to cheer,
    my father holds binoculars
        to my mother's eyes.
I won't breathe until he lands,
    my brother, black
        as an eighth note drifting
against the sky.

SOMETHING FOR MARVIN

used to be

that skull cap

& peasy peasy beard

w/ grapevine whines.

       But it was style

a new sound smooth

as the motor's croon in Motortown.

Style like Fat Bone's

Caddy cruising

down Blackbird street.

used to be

that tuxedo

& greasy, greasy hair

w/ sexual

healin squealin

       But it was style

a sound

tellin as the engine's hum

on weekdays,

Fat Bone wore his workpants,

the caddy wasn't washed,

but still it hummed

like field hands.

Suit. Dark suit so easy

w/ those flowers. *Lord's*

Lost Him His mockingbird

  The mourners moan like lovers

pinched in some shiny black splendor

        I want my father to kill me,

& use my blood for fuel.

        I want to live forever

like the singer resurrected

in the record's groove.

GOLIATH POEM

I am always sorry for the big ape falling

from the Empire for love. Or Esau, a big man,

begging his father for even a breadcrumb

of thy Grace— sly brother-Jacob scampering

off to seed a nation. Dudes like that.

All muscle and hands weeping on the shoulder

of regret, which is a kind of blindness,

a recognition come too late. Sometimes I am sorry

for Rick, whom I love, where ever he may be,

six-foot eight hurling stones through the window

of another woman who's turned him away,

and I too far this time to drive to him in the night.

Who will save the big men of this world?

Earlier I watched *King Kong* and was sorry again

for those building-size fuckers we see falling

from miles away. Those we thought invincible,

almost permanent like the sun which burns,

truthfully, only a few hours each day.

Once when his girlfriend called me, I drove in the rain

from college to his house. Nintendo cords roped

his shoes, a bottle of pills between his thighs, he sat

on the couch. In the darkness we could have been the same.

Perhaps I thought of holding him, my twin,

or thought of another door and my father weeping

beyond it a month before. I could have talked

about the horse on its carousel; how each man lowers

his head to circle, blindly, his life. But we said nothing.

We listened to rain like the sound of a big man's tears,

the sound God made before the Word or Light,

And the moon curved above us like an ear.

NOIR: ORPHEUS

Liberty Avenue emptied long ago,
Though a few white-hair businessmen hustle
Along the sidewalk wrapped in aluminum-
Colored suits; their briefcases black as Bibles.
There are shadows hugging in the alley.
Everywhere the big-hand homeless reach.

And there's me, rookie night-freak,
Asking the clerk for a booth.
Finding you, like the last cookie
In a cracked display case.

Here I am, Baby,
Pushing quarters into a slot
To keep you dancing,
My silent, sleepy-eyed Eurydice.

Here we are, Baby.
Fuck the college boys clutching in the hallway.
Fuck this oddly placed napkin dispenser.
You are pure as the water bottle in the corner,
You are mysterious as the crosswords on the floor.

I should be looking at you, I know:

Your lips red as a matador's cape;

How you bend and open

Like a girl pretending to be a flower;

But I don't love you. I don't love my eyes.

How not think of Orpheus

Dragging his wife from Hell—

A few steps from sunlight,

Betrayed by his own ravenous glare.

Love should be a tow truck—

What rescues our stalled, abandoned hearts;

What leads us back to repair.

Love should save us,

But it won't.

SOME LUMINOUS DISTRESS

for Betty Shabazz

Not even tomorrow morning can save us—
Not even this great American space,
Palatial and white with stars can save me

Or the burning house engines holler
Off to douse: curtains flaring at the windows
Like hair, the black woman locked

In bright sleep—None of it.
Yea, though I walk this stone
Unraveling valley, I shall fear no evil. Do I follow

The siren, the men with red hats
And hoses— angels on their chariot,
The yawn of smoke there—

Just over the hill; some luminous distress?
Why not burn, star bright? I fear no evil,
Nor good will guide me. Only this night

Which takes my eyes, these limbs
Shedding their secrets,
Young scabs falling from wounds.

How else do I say it? The leaves

      Are falling. Three blocks from here:

The flame, and somewhere else, the white-

      Palmed child who set it. Do you see

How smoke & absence can blow

      The heart from its branch? Sunday's over,

It's Fall. Only softskin sinners

      And the butterbean moon; the siren's

Dirge just over the hill, the lit sky,

      The limbs black against it.

Where is my shepard and his rod?

      Yea, though I walk...   Where ever

This night is headed, I'll follow,

      Where ever I'm going, I've been.

LATE

for my mother

This late, no one is clean,

not the bus's worn blue seats

which keep themselves company,

or the nurse in her drowsy yellow uniform.

It's February and I haven't spoken

to my mother since she told me

to take my shit and go, her face

bare and serious as a wall.

The driver waves a gloved hand

at a passing bus, slow and half empty

like us. Heads of the riders turned

so that I cannot say how they appear.

I was not born in this place,

but it is where I will try to live. The miles

between my mother and here, stretching me

into more of a man than my father,

who'd drive from his out of state job

each weekend to let her break his skin.

I am glad I have left her sitting in that house

waiting for her nails to grow.

Once she pulled a gun on me because,

as she'd tell the police, I was too big

for a belt. I called them, but they did not

take her away. Later, my father drove home

and said, *Never put our business in the street.*

So I shouldn't be telling you this:

how we sat in that house like a family

while a small light beat the blinds,

my mother stubborn as a girl

who will not comb her hair.

There is no light beyond the windows

of this bus. I am given my face,

transparent and bare on the glass.

After my father left that night,

the two of us sat apart in the living-room

as the t.v. lit the walls, the old white gown

trembling on her shoulders like the wings

of a moth. I will say I did not know

she began to cry. I was 18, trying to be

a man. It has taken me too long to say this,

I am the same thing I have always been,

a son. I do not know my mother,

but I want to touch her now, as I did not then.

TENDERNESS

For it is all or nothing in this life, for there is no other.
    —Larry Levis

It does not stop. It does not stop until you are safely home,
Smoking the cigarette you will not finish and watching snow
Which does not stop parade outside the window.
You have rummaged the mail for a letter
From the woman you wish was your lover, thin loop of her name
Flowering the envelope, but it was not there.
You have gone through the house opening everything:
The refrigerator, its bare white space, then the cabinets' black
      caskets,
Then the poetry book, & finally the army jacket
Which could not warm you in the cold.
It was your father's. His name embroidered black on the pocket
You let people think your own.
What did the old man ask in the grocery store: *Patriot?*
What was that look as you backed from his face
And told him it wasn't yours?

But now you are with the book which cannot be enough,
Dialing Nancy to read her words too good to be your own;
Her doe voice wavering in the electric reel of the answering
      machine.

"I had some Levis to read you," you say imagining her straining

To hear your music in the background, then erasing the

message.

You wanted her to hear the part where the poet speaks

Of love & passion. . . *Any nakedness, the first time I saw it then,*

Was still wonder. Even now, as you read it to yourself, it tells

you tenderness

Is possible, is in the world, though earlier you said otherwise.

It was her admitting she wanted to cry but not crying,

A separate grief shaking free, then lodged again in her throat.

There was tenderness.

It was you who went in your camouflage jacket to the door,

To the snow falling on Pittsburgh, on Forbes Avenue,

the city's ghosts.

Yes, move, for a moment, away from tenderness.

It was you who thought of Billy Stayhorn's *Lush Life*

Written when he was nineteen beneathe this very sky,

Still the color of Andrew Carnegie's beard, still dragging

Men home by the collar, *girls with sad and sullen gray faces.* . . .

Whatever the song says, whatever Levis says,

Each is the same message you will chariot through the week.

You should have held that woman. A brief embrace,

That would have been tenderness.

You should have held your father when he gave you his coat

   & went away.

That would have been tenderness.   . . . *all or nothing in this life.*

   There is no other.

The cigarette is half finished,

Breathing alone in the tray. The snow has eased its report.

I know one of the rings of Hell is for men who refuse to weep.

So I let it come. And it does not move from me.

BLACKBIRD
(Calling My Brother To Hear Roberta)

She was the blackbird in our house,
Full of color and song like that.

My mother asleep on the couch,
My brother at his books,

I'd lock the bedroom door
To sing her Siren songs,

Let our music loop the room,
Flutter against the walls all night.

And I wanted a woman to someday
Make me feel like that,

Something better than orgasm or God,
Deeper than spoken words.

I wished for a woman's shoes
Tipped like blackbirds beside my bed,

Her bra, soft halves of a blackbird shell.
I wished for a woman's blackbird scent

And her blackbird touch beside my own.

I wished to always be in love.

Tonight, Roberta sings

Across nine hours of telephone lines,

And when I close my eyes, my mouth

Flings open like a June window.

In this empty room, her song unlocks

The wing of my silent tongue.

LADY SINGS THE BLUES

Satin luscious, amber Beauty center-stage;
      gardenia in her hair. If flowers could sing
they'd sound like this. That legendary scene:
      the lady unpetals her song, the only light

in a room of smoke, nightclub tinkering
      with lovers in the dark, cigarette flares,
gin & tonic. This is where the heartache
      blooms. Forget the holes

zippered along her arms. Forget the booze.
      Center-stage, satin-tongue dispels a note.

Amber amaryllis, blue chanteuse, Amen.
      If flowers could sing they'd sound like this.

———————————

This should be Harlem, but it's not.
      It's Diana Ross with no *Supremes*.
Fox Theater, Nineteen Seventy-something.
      Ma and me; lovers crowded in the dark.

The only light breaks on the movie-screen.
      I'm a boy, but old enough to know *Heartache*.

We watch her rise and wither

      like a burnt-out cliche. You know the story:

Brutal lush. Jail-bird. Scag queen.

      In the asylum scene, the actress's eyes

are bruised; latticed with blood, but not quite sad

         enough. She's the star so her beauty persists.

Not like Billie: fucked-up satin, hair museless,

      heart ruined by the end.

      ————————————

The houselights wake and nobody's blue but Ma.

      Billie didn't sound like that, she says

as we walk hand in hand to the street.

      Nineteen Seventy-something,

My lady hums, *Good Morning Heartache,*

      My father's in a distant place.

POET DYING AT THE WINDOW

I have a goddamn for every blade

of snow. You're not even to the road

before it's clinging to your coat.

Said I wouldn't write anymore

about matters of the heart,

so I'm writing about the snow—

God's cryogenic rain; cold trick/le

of repetition falling quietly as ghosts.

Is this what Etheridge meant?

Walls blacker than a throat;

Poet dying at the window;

Flakes/ covering your tracks as you go.

(Mr. Mouse Plays the Blues)

I lov-   ove

e you, I l-   you,

these whispers zip

like mice

      thru a labyrinth and, Baby,

                       my brain

               is a labyrinth,

because this love's no simple thing, no

           marginal thing,

it boasts past the borders

            of nonsense,

      the Mason-Dixie line of logic.

I love you I love you I love you,

say it again and again

Love, say, is a cat with black stripes.

All week past the man alone in bed, it hunts

idle mice. SCRAM! SCRAPE! THWACK!

aHH, Love,

the word makes me

want to put on my shoes

and walk, but

      I sit listening

to the stereo that squats in the corner

        like a block of cheese,

and your leaving makes sense

according to the Blues:

      so-longs & slow notes

spilling the air you dwelt,

mixing like a cocktail

        til I'm too drunk,

   and dizzy

      as a '45.

(Lord, the words

     are never enough)

Crickety,

    scratch,

      shiver...

Is that crazy cat

   at the door again:

my electric invisible,

     my moonlight dim,

(crackle) (shBoom)

     (kaPuff)!

my imaginary

   something?

Come in, Kitty-cat, come in.

HATHAWAY

...close your eyes and think of me....

— *"You've Got A Friend,"*
  Roberta Flack & Donny Hathaway Duets

You close your eyes

& join them.

I say, "Remember

Donny Hathaway's suicide?"

He was a brown note falling

Fifteen stories the winter of '79.

All that music gone.

I almost say how hard it hit

My father. You're singing,

   Where ever I am, I'll come running...

Once I caught a janitor singing

In the bathroom. Not words.

Just a lyric-jumble

Above the squash of mop water.

I want to tell you
How I told him; to shut up

How my father's baritone
Covered me like a shirt,

I want to hold off the music a while.
After Donny, I say,   All the music

Withered from Roberta's tongue.
She stumbled on stage later

That summer & sang
So awful, my father said,

It had to be about loss.
I want to say, Anything beautiful

Cracks into silence,
but you won't stop

Singing. Humming,
when the words run out.

WOMAN WALKING ON THE ROAD

We were in the car. We were heading home when Christian
with his wholly American name & manic chatter told his
    girlfriend
the woman we saw walking on the road with no umbrella
was a symbol of torment.We were in the backseat—
you with that face making the windows & the black world
beyond the windows beautiful, the roadside figure of a woman
in the rain beautiful & I knew later I'd be writing these lines,
caught in that space between personal & public:
a woman's torment or symbol of it & our love & goddamn
everybody's sins scribbled here for show. We were in the car
heading home when Christian said the woman on the road
was probably fresh from a fight with her husband,
but he didn't say his fists gave his last girlfriend bruises
& I didn't say it either... The woman was walking alone
on the shoulder & meant something different & utterly the same
to each of us— her lit up life & husband left looking
from a window, as I have looked from a window, guilty.
But Guilt ain't nobody's business. We were in the car, we saw
a woman walking on the road. There was a woman who,
after our quarrels, would steal my car, a little blue Datsun
with a dented fender. She'd drive from our dorm to the blank
    streets
of the town we lived in; she'd drive past the empty classrooms,

the soccer field, to God knows where & I wanted her, then,

away from me— two red lights, a tired engine leaving smoke.

But one night I groped in the darkness beneathe my hood

until I disconnected something & if there is such a thing

      as malice,

that was it— a man sabotaging his own car so his lover

      couldn't run...

I'm shaking my head because I want to say I'm different now,

like Christian— someone with a new face beside him & a pain

no one can see, perhaps, settled in his chest. Your new face

beside me. I am damaged, I have bruised. We fought over

      something

stupid & she came so close I knew she could smell my blood.

Have I come far enough to say I hit her; to say my hand left

      a cloud

on her cheek? Have I come far enough to say, I'm sorry?

      We were

in the car, you with that face making the windows & the world

beyond the windows real; the figure of a woman on the road

telling the truth. Once in my small brutal past a woman left me,

walked from my lit up fingers to the street with a storm

      on her face.

It was raining. I watched from the window & could not follow,

my car sat in the lot disconnected, unopened, unmoved.

WHEN THE NEIGHBORS FIGHT,

The trumpet's mouth is apology.

    We sit listening

To *Kind of Blue*. Miles Davis

    Beat his wife. It hurts

To know the music is better

    Than him. The wall

Is damaged skin. Tears can purify

    The heart. Even the soft

Kiss can bite. Miles Davis beat

    His wife. It's muffled

In the jazz, the struggle

    With good & bad. The wall

Is damaged skin. The horn knows

    A serious fear.

Your tongue burns pushing

    Into my ear. Miles Davis

Beat his wife. No one called
    The cops until the music

Stopped. The heart is a muted
    Horn. The horn is a bleeding

Wife. Our neighbors are a score
    Of danger. You open

My shirt like doors you want
    To enter. I am tender

As regret. Mouth on the nipple
    Above my heart.

There is the good pain
    Of your bite.

MIDNIGHT,

you call
Minutes before the train

Weaves you deeper
Into the gut of San Francisco

To say a new sun
Is tattooed on your shoulder

I imagine it burning
Down my throat

At the airport,
I saw a woman's fingers

Play the neck
Of her husband

I don't remember their faces
I have forgotten everything

But the sound of distance
I had not touched

Myself for months
Before now

BOXCAR

for John & Miles, together

Black as snow & ice as cool/ Miles stood horn-handed while
John so&soloed/ I mean mad but mute like you be when you
got five minutes/ to be somewhere ten minutes away & a train
outta nowhere stops you/ boxcarboxcarboxcar & tracknoise/
that might out shout your radio if you had your windows
down/ boxcarboxcar & hotcars lined up around you/this is
how mad Miles was/ Impatient like his dentist daddy/ listenin
to a badmouth whine about some aching pain/ *See, Doc I was*
tryin to blow down my old lady's door / Theres Miles listenin/ to
Johns long song about sufferin & loss/ & hes heard it all before
in a club in the village/ He standin horn-handed but the
jazzfolk sit lovin it/ cause it all sounds new as sunday
shoes/ / Ticked Miles checks his watch/ tickles his trumpet/
& listens to a muscular music that wont stop/ & he loves it or
maybe he scared nobody will ever hear him again/ or maybe he
hungry & want to get/ home to silence/John got nowhere but
here/ got nothin but this/ cause his wifes asleep/ & she cant
give him this kind of love/ his lips swoll as carolina clay/
almost bleedin on the reed & its just what he wants/ Blood/ / &
when he finally hush/ dead years later/ his liver rotten as corn
& Naimas gone/ Miles aint even glad its over/ His ears full of
whats left him/ & he thinkin of black hands dancin like
crowswings/ & he thinkin of a lovesupreme a lovesupreme a
lovesupreme/& this too is what Im thinkin/ as I drive to see my
diva/ with old jazz in my speakers & the only thing between us
these boxcars pullin & pullin & pullin past

NOTES

SOMETHING FOR MARVIN
Marvin Gaye was killed by his father in 1984. A line in the poem
is taken from Robert Hayden's "Mourning Poem for the Queen
of Sunday."

> Lord's lost Him His Mockingbird,
>
> His fancy warbler;
>
> Satan sweet-talked her,
>
> four bullets hushed her.
>
> Who would have thought
>
> she'd end that way?

TENDERNESS
Lines in the poem are taken from poems in Larry Levis' book,
The Widening Spell Of Leaves and Billy Strayhorn's song,
"Lush Life."

POET DYING AT THE WINDOW
The poem makes a reference to lines from Etheridge Knight's
poem: "As You Leave Me."

BOXCAR
The poem was inspired by the story about John Coltrane's
notoriously long solos in the years he played with the Miles
Davis Quartet. When Miles reportedly asked him why he
always played so long, John answered, "When I start, I don't
know how to stop."

"Just take the damn horn out of your mouth," Miles told him.